Amazon FBA 2019

How to Create and Manage a Successful

E-Commerce Business Step by Step

By: Dale McLeo

Table of Contents

Introduction

Amazon FBA or fulfillment by Amazon is a business opportunity that offers people the opportunity to operate their own e-commerce store without having to deal with all of the technical bells and whistles that can make traditional e-commerce seem daunting.

If you desire to run your own e-commerce store, Amazon FBA is a wonderful way for you to get started. This unique business opportunity presents you with so many benefits that you simply will not gain elsewhere, making e-commerce easier to get into than ever before. The abundance of benefits that you gain with this opportunity means that you can run your Amazon FBA store as a full-time gig without having to put in full-time hours. Countless people have been able to make $10,000+ per month using this platform, all the while being able to enjoy their lives and time freedom due to the hands-off structure of this business.

That's right! Because of how Amazon FBA works, you actually do not have to invest that much time into your business to start and maintain it. While it will take some practice and effort early on to get started and get your business going, maintaining and even scaling your business with Amazon FBA takes significantly less time than it would with nearly any other business model. This means that not only are you going to be able to turn a great profit, but you are also going to be able to actually have time to enjoy that profit you are turning so that you can really live your best life!

In this book, I want to support you with discovering all of the ins and outs of Amazon FBA. I am going to help you discover exactly what this business model is, how it works, and what you need to do in order to leverage it. I am also going to help you identify how you can set yourself apart from the others who are using Amazon FBA by supporting you with discovering the right products to sell, as well as the right brand to use to actually sell those products. By blending together all of the tips and techniques I give you in this very book, you are going to have all of the knowledge that you need to make your business work.

The best way to use this book so that you can actually gain that level of success is to start by reading this book cover-to-cover so that you know exactly what is going to be required of you for you to succeed. Then, once you have a clear outline in your mind, you can go back through this book and follow the process step-by-step as directed within these very chapters. Using this method is going to help you have the best blueprint for success both on paper and in your mind so that you can really leverage your knowledge to succeed.

If you are ready to begin the journey of launching your own Amazon FBA business, it's time to begin. I encourage you to really take your time with this book and follow all the cues as they arise, as this is going to ensure that you follow the exact blueprint to build your successful Amazon FBA business. And, of course, please enjoy!

Chapter 1: Introduction To Amazon FBA

Amazon FBA is a business model that was originally presented by Amazon back in 2006. At the time, Amazon wanted to help it's merchants along by providing warehouses that their merchants could ship their supplies to, allowing Amazon employees to be responsible for everything related to product shipments. This meant that merchants would order products and have them delivered to specific Amazon warehouses, where Amazon would then package and ship the products for those merchants. Amazon would also manage returns and exchanges, and anything else related to managing the products for their merchants.

Amazon FBA was introduced as part of Amazon's initiative to remain at the forefront of e-commerce growth. However, it was not until recent years that this business model truly began to mature and take off. Although people were using Amazon FBA in the past, the cost to get involved in such a modality was still fairly large for the average person. While Amazon did their best to make their features accessible, wholesalers and other suppliers were still fairly expensive to purchase from which meant that you would still require a large start-up fund if you were going to get involved with this practice.

Fortunately, with the spike in popularity for e-commerce in recent years, this has completely changed. Within the past decade, more wholesalers and merchants have become available for those wanting to get started in e-commerce, many of which have accessible and affordable entry points for the average person. This has made it far more feasible for people to get involved with e-commerce, especially once you factor in the benefits of a platform like Amazon FBA.

In this chapter, I want to help give you a clear look on what selling with Amazon FBA looks like so that you can see exactly what you are getting into when you begin to sell with this platform.

Selling Rules And Guidelines

Amazon FBA has a series of rules and guidelines that help protect the platform, as well as the sellers who are using the platform. These rules and guidelines typically pertain to the legal structure of the business to ensure that everyone is being reasonable in how they are using the platform, and no one is getting into any legal trouble.

Below is an outline of each of the important policies and requirements that you need to know about selling on Amazon FBA as of 2019.

Customer Feedback

All orders shipped through Amazon FBA are subjected to customer feedback. If a customer leaves feedback that negatively reflects the shipping or order fulfillment, that does not count against your seller rating as Amazon owns full responsibility for that.

Customer Returns

Amazon FBA has its own return policy that determines whether a product is eligible to be returned or exchanged. The seller does not have the right to determine what these guidelines are. However, they are obligated to provide the partial or full refund funds should Amazon FBA deem the product is eligible for a refund.

Customer Service with Multi-Channel Fulfillment Orders

Multi-channel fulfillment means that you are selling your products on platforms beyond Amazon. With Amazon FBA, only products that are registered through your Amazon FBA and shipped to the facility itself and then sold on Amazon will be fulfilled. All sales that are completed elsewhere, such as on your own private website, will need to be fulfilled and managed by you. Amazon does not support this fulfillment structure in any way.

Lost and Damaged Inventory Reimbursement

If Amazon is responsible for damaging or losing your inventory, they will provide you with a full or partial refund depending on the amount of product that has been lost or damaged. If, however, Amazon is not responsible for the damage or loss (such as if it happens in transport or at the warehouse of your supplier) they will not reimburse you. You will need to speak with your supplier or transport company for support with that.

Product Restrictions

Certain products, particularly those with expiration dates or that may be temperature sensitive, may not be eligible to be sold through Amazon FBA. If you are selling anything that may require special storage or shipment requirements, you will need to contact Amazon FBA to see if that product is eligible. If you are selling products that are considered dangerous goods, alcoholic beverages (including non-alcoholic beer,) vehicle tires, floating lanterns, gift cards or gift certificates, or products that require specific licensing to sell, they are also not eligible. As well, anything that has been illegally replicated or manufactured, that does not comply with the legal agreement between Amazon and their sellers, or that has not been properly registered with Amazon FBA will not be eligible for Amazon FBA sales.

Important Features To Know About

Amazon FBA has a variety of different features that make running your business convenient and relatively simple. Although there will be a learning curve, as there is with anything, once you discover how to use this platform, you will find that it is extremely simple.

The first and obvious feature that comes with Amazon FBA is inventory management and shipping fulfillment. Amazon employees will receive your orders from your supplier, check for their quality, and manage the inventory in their own warehouse, leaving you completely out of the equation. Other than ordering your products and having them shipped to the warehouse, all you need to do is monitor status updates on your seller account to ensure that everything is running smoothly. When a product is ordered, Amazon employees will ship that product and manage all shipping-related concerns until the product has been received by your client. Should any returns or exchanges be required, Amazon will manage that, too.

Amazon FBA also offers discounted shipping rates because they have their own shipping contracts in place. Due to the massive volume of products that they are always shipping, they are able to score a far greater deal than you will ever be able to get for yourself as an individual running one single business. This means that you are going to be able to save your clients a great deal of money, and save yourself a great deal, too. Another great benefit of this shipping set up is that your orders will be shipped much faster and will reach your client sooner because they are able to access Amazon's 2-day shipping feature.

In fact, it's not just the 2-day shipping feature that is being unlocked. *All* Amazon Prime features will be unlocked for your store. This means that anytime someone shops with you, they will access all of the benefits of Amazon Prime, ranging from fast and free shipping to priority service. As the seller, you also receive access to special promotional benefits on Amazon itself as Amazon promotes Amazon Prime-enabled stores to their members more to provide them with a better shopping experience.

In addition to Amazon Prime features, you and your clients also gain access to 24/7 customer service. Amazon employees are on-call through phone support, chat support, and e-mail support at all hours of the day, every day of the week to provide you and your clients with priority service if you ever require support. This feature alone is an incredibly valuable feature that frees up a lot of time and energy from your schedule so that you are not sitting around waiting for and managing customer service inquiries all day.

Although standard Amazon FBA features do not allow for multi-channel fulfillment features, there is a feature that you can pay for that allows you to access multi-channel fulfillment as well. If you set up an Amazon FBA account with this feature activated, you do access the opportunity to run your e-commerce store elsewhere on the net while still having all of your orders being fulfilled by Amazon FBA. This means that you can run a massive online empire, all the while having Amazon behind all of your shipping and customer service features. If you are looking to scale your e-commerce business as large as possible, this is an important feature to know about.

Finally, Amazon has hundreds of warehouses all over North America that are devoted to Amazon FBA. This means that if you are looking to grow a massive empire, you can access virtually unlimited storage space for all of your products. Unlimited growth means that there is no cap on how far you can go with your business, granting you the opportunity to just keep growing and earning a bigger profit month over month. If you are looking for a long-term opportunity that is going to help you score a huge income, Amazon FBA is a great opportunity.

How Selling Works

Selling on Amazon FBA works differently from other e-commerce platforms since you are more hands-off than you are with other platforms. Whereas on other platforms you would need to receive shipments, check for quality, organize your inventory, manage your inventory, ship your inventory, manage your shipments, manage customer service, and manage feedback, you do not with Amazon FBA. All of these features are covered for you in the selling process, which makes your contributions much simpler and more convenient. That being said, there are still things that need to take place on your end for sales to actually happen, and that is important to know about. Although this process is a lot easier, it is not entirely hands-off, which means you are still going to have some level of involvement in order to turn your store into a massive success.

As the seller, there are three primary things that you need to pay attention to in order to make sales: what products you are selling, how you are advertising them, and what feedback you are receiving. These three areas are going to help you structure your sales so that you are able to get the most sales possible, allowing you to grow your store rapidly.

In terms of what products you are selling, you need to ensure that your store has the right products to attract people in the first place. If you are not selling the right products, your clients are not going to come because they are not going to be interested in what you have to offer them. Picking the right products and the right price points is crucial.

Advertising happens in many ways and is generally a lot easier than it may sound. With advertising, you want to focus on getting the word out there, establishing a recognizable brand, and leveraging behind-the-scenes features like SEO so that you can get seen. We will discuss all of this in greater detail later on so that you know exactly how to navigate these features, or how to outsource them if you wish to have someone else running the marketing portion of your store in the future.

You also need to pay attention to the feedback that you are receiving from your customers so that you know how to grow your store. Feedback is going to tell you what your customers like, what they don't like, and what they want to see more of. Even something as basic as someone rating your products without saying a single word about them can be valuable in helping you choose the direction of your products and brand, which you will learn about later as well.

Once you learn to navigate and manage these three parts of selling, getting your products into the hands of customers is easy. All you have to do is remain consistent and continue taking advantage of the features that are available to you for you to grow your business and make consistent sales day in and day out.

Amazon FBA Fee Structure

As you can probably expect, a feature like Amazon FBA is certainly not free. You are going to have to pay to access all of these features, which is something that you need to be fully aware of. Understanding Amazon FBA's fee structure will ensure that you are aware of what you will be spending going into your business, which will prove to be incredibly helpful in the future when you are determining what products to sell. It will also help you discover what your profits are and how your store is growing.

Amazon FBA has two primary fees that you are going to be paying: fulfillment fees and monthly storage fees.

Fulfillment fees are fees that you pay every single time an order is placed, and when some orders are returned or exchanged unless they are on Amazon's specific "free customer returns" category. These fees vary depending on the size of the product and how much it weighs, as well as what type of product it is.

The current fee structure is as follows:

Small (1lb or less)	$2.41	Small Oversize (2lb+)	$8.13 + .38c per additional lb
Medium (1lb or less)	$3.19	Medium Oversize (2lb+)	$9.44 + .38c per additional lb
Large (1-2lb)	$4.71	Large Oversize (90lb+)	$73.18 + .79c per additional lb
Special (Over 2lb)	$4.71 + .38c per additional lb	Special Oversize (90lb+)	$137.32 + .91c per additional lb

Monthly storage fees are fees that you pay to store your products at Amazon's warehouses. These fees are based on how many cubic feet you are occupying in Amazon's warehouse with your products. As long as you have products at their warehouse, you will be paying this fee each month.

The current monthly storage fee structure is as follows:

Months Stored	Standard-Sized Products	Oversized Products
January-September	.64c per cubic foot	.43c per cubic foot
October-December	$2.35 per cubic foot	$1.15 per cubic foot

There are special fees that will be paid on all orders that are fulfilled through channels other than Amazon's platform, which vary depending on the product size and type. You can discover fees related to your specific products on Amazon's website through your FBA seller's account.

Chapter 2: Planning For Success

The first step in generating success in any business is planning. If you want to have success with Amazon FBA, this is no different. You need to be prepared to plan for success through having the right mindset and the right business plan to win with. In this chapter, we are going to explore how both your mindset and your practical business plan will contribute to your success, and how you can ensure that both are on track for your success.

Planning For The Right Mindset

If you look at any successful business owner, their mindset is entirely different from that of the average person. This is true for every form of business owner, including those who are running businesses on e-commerce platforms like Amazon with Amazon FBA. Your mindset is responsible for supporting you with your ability to keep going even when it feels tough or like you are struggling to really get anywhere with your business. Having the right mindset is going to help you succeed faster, earn more, and scale your business bigger in a shorter amount of time. For many people, mindset is the difference between persisting until you win or quitting before you even have a chance.

With Amazon FBA, your mindset is what is going to help you see your success before your bank account does, and that level of faith and commitment to making it work is crucial. This is where you are going to find the drive and inspiration to keep going so that you can find the right path forward for your business, no matter what obstacle or challenge you may face along the way.

For an entrepreneurial mindset, there are five main tips that you need to know to help you get started.

Take Advice From The Right People

As you go into the process of growing your Amazon FBA business, knowing how to take advice from other people is going to be crucial. When it comes to mindset, being willing to take advice and find ways to grow your business through the support of others is also known as having a "growth mindset." This essentially means that you are willing to listen to other people and receive guidance from them that is going to help you achieve maximum growth in your own business.

Getting advice from others requires two important pieces from your end. Willingness to receive and act on advice is one crucial part of the process so that you can stay open to receiving what you learn from others. The other part is knowing how to make sure that you are taking advice from the right people so that you are getting the information that you need to grow. When it comes to developing your business and growing to the point that you want to, knowing how to screen people to ensure that they are the right person to learn from is crucial. If you take advice from the wrong people, you may find yourself confused or making decisions that are ultimately not ideal for the growth of your business.

As a general rule of thumb, never take advice from people who are not actively experiencing the level of success that you want to experience. Although you can certainly receive alternative opinions and points of view from others, you should only truly take advice from those who are already where you want to be. That is because these are the people who know what it takes to get there and who can give you the advice that actually worked, from the point of view of someone who made it work. The key here is that these individuals will not only explain it to you, but they can also tell you what to pay attention to so that you can maximize your growth and minimize your risk. They know exactly what the potential troubles you may run into would be, how to see them coming, and what to do if you find yourself in these situations. Someone who has not already been through the growth and achieved the success that you want to achieve would not be at this point yet. Therefore, they would be incapable of offering you the best advice possible to get you where you want to go.

Promote Yourself Frequently

If you have ever done any self-development work around mindset, you know that the way you talk to yourself has a massive impact on how you live your life. People who talk nicely to themselves and about themselves tend to be happier overall, have an easier time growing, and are more open to life and all of the trials and opportunities that life has to offer. Alternatively, people who talk rudely to themselves and about themselves find that they are miserable, have low self-confidence and self-esteem, and generally feel like they are incapable of achieving anything in their lives. Often, they feel as though they are being trampled by life and the natural obstacles and challenges that people generally face in their lives.

In order to grow as an entrepreneur and give yourself the best opportunity to succeed, you need to be willing to have a positive mindset toward yourself and a positive attitude toward promoting yourself. Talking nicely to yourself and about yourself when it comes to your capabilities and qualifications and when it comes to talking about your business is an excellent opportunity for you to grow your presence and achieve higher levels of growth. After all, how is anyone going to be able to learn about you and your business if you refuse to talk about yourself, or if you play it down like your business is not that big of a deal?

To help make it easier for you to promote yourself to others, it is a good idea for you to start by promoting yourself to yourself. Learn how to talk to yourself in a way that promotes what you do, and that makes your success seem incredible to yourself. Get comfortable with raving to yourself about how great your business is, how awesome your products are, and how incredible you are at serving your audience in the best way possible. This way, you are preparing yourself for what it feels like to talk about and listen to these nice things being said about you and your business. Ultimately, this is going to help you boost your self-confidence and self-esteem, and help you find new ways to promote yourself to others.

Once you grow more confident in promoting yourself to yourself, you need to start shamelessly promoting yourself to others! Learn how to cultivate charisma and tact when promoting yourself, and then go ahead and speak away. Let people know what you have going on, explain what you are doing to them, and give them opportunities to find you online so that they can shop with your business. This level of confidence and charisma will be a massive help in supporting you with growing your business through networking and connecting with those who are likely to be interested in purchasing from your business in the first place.

Leverage Your Strengths In Business

In any business that you are a part of, whether its Amazon FBA or anything else, knowing how to identify and leverage your strengths is a crucial opportunity for you to grow faster. Every single person has strengths, and strengths of all shapes and sizes can contribute to the success of your business. Finding out what your strengths are and learning how you can leverage those to help you grow your business is a great opportunity for you to excel in your growth.

A great example of leveraging your strengths will be if you are exceptional with scheduling and ordering. A punctual person is incredible at getting everything done on time, which means that you are going to excel with Amazon FBA because you can ensure that your orders are always submitted delivered to the warehouse on time. If you find that punctuality is your strength, you can always create a strong schedule that is going to help you submit everything on time so that your business is flourishing.

If you find that ordering and managing the backend of things is your strength but punctuality is not, then you might adapt the way that you do things differently. In this case, you might prepare all of your orders and shipments in advance so that you do not find yourself scrambling at the last minute to get everything done. This way, you are confident that you are prepared to get your products to the warehouse on time every time, ensuring that you always have plenty of stock for your customers to order.

In addition to knowing what your strengths are and leveraging them, you should also be aware of what your weaknesses are. Having a clear understanding of what you might struggle with or where you might fall flat in your business can help you use your strengths to offset these weaknesses and keep you going strong. If you cannot fully offset them, at least you can be aware of them and plan for you to have plenty of time to navigate all of the tasks relating to these weaknesses so that you are always running your business steadily. You can also plan to learn new skills and techniques to help these weaknesses less of a burden so that you can still run your business efficiently and without any unnecessary troubles.

Build Your Network

Entrepreneurs value greatly from having a strong network, yet it is common for people who are in the entrepreneurial world to isolate themselves and attempt to do everything alone. For many entrepreneurs, they behave as if they have something to prove, and so, they struggle to really get ahead in their businesses because they are always trying to balance everything on their own shoulders. Although this may feel like the way you have to do things, trust that this is not the best solution and that growing your network and having support truly is the best way to go forward. This does not mean that you need to bring on any business partners or investors to succeed, but it does mean that you should have a strong network of people who can support you in cultivating success in your journey.

Building your network as an entrepreneur requires you to build out your network in a strategic way where you will be connected with people who can help you, and people who you can help in return. Doing this will ensure that all of your connections are mutually beneficial and able to be nurtured so that you have a maximum chance of achieving success in your business.

As you build your network, seek to grow with people who are also selling on Amazon FBA, as well as other retailers and entrepreneurs. Never discredit the value of someone simply because they are not doing exactly what you are doing, as everyone who is actively running a business has the capacity to give you some level of knowledge around what you are doing. Whether they can support you with having greater success in advertising, or help you upload products to your Amazon FBA shop and sell them, everyone can support you in one way or another. The key is to make sure that you understand *why* you are adding everyone to your network and what value you can gain from them so that you always know why you might talk to them and what advice you should be receiving from them. If anyone from your network tries to give you advice about something that seems to be out of their realm of expertise, always validate that advice with someone else who you would consider to be an expert. This way, you can always feel confident about the advice that you are gaining from the people in your network.

Always Keep Learning

As I mentioned with gaining advice from others, a growth mindset is crucial to your success. People with a growth mindset tend to be more open to receiving advice, are willing to find solutions to the problems they may be facing, and frequently look at life as a series of opportunities and lessons rather than a series of setbacks and failures. If you want to have the right mindset to succeed with your business, you need to always keep learning.

Look for opportunities to improve your mindset, to learn more about your Amazon FBA business, and to learn more about advertising and business in general. Stay open-minded to ways that you can follow the trends in your industry and be willing to adapt your plan accordingly if you see new opportunities to improve your growth. The more willing and open you are, the more you are going to spot the growth opportunities with your business, and therefore, the more growth you are going to achieve. Growth mindset and a willingness to stay open to learning is something that virtually all entrepreneurs who achieve massive success in their businesses have in common.

Planning For A Successful Business

In addition to preparing your mindset for the growth that you wish to achieve, you also need to plan for success in your business. Planning for a successful business comes *after* cultivating the right mindset because, this way, you can feel confident that you are going into the process with a willingness to learn all that there is to know in order for you to succeed. Below I am going to give you five key steps for you to know exactly what you are planning for and how you can plan for it so that you can achieve the greatest success possible with your business.

Know What You Are Planning

First things first, you have to know what you are planning. Knowing that you want to plan to develop an Amazon FBA business is a great first step in getting started. However, you need to be prepared to go even further than that. You need to know exactly what all of the steps are that go into planning an Amazon FBA business so that you are clear on exactly what actions need to be accommodated for in your plan, allowing you to achieve maximum success.

Throughout this very book, you are going to be discovering the key steps that go into planning an Amazon FBA business, so this is a great place to start. However, in order to give you a general overview right now so that you do not have to wait so long to put all of the pieces together, I have outlined the process for you below.

Here is what you will need to plan for when it comes to growing your Amazon FBA business:

- Choose to start your Amazon FBA business
- Identify how Amazon FBA works and educate yourself on the process
- Open your Amazon FBA seller account
- Brand your Amazon FBA store
- Discover what products you want to sell
- Source your products and have them approved by Amazon FBA
- Ship your products to Amazon FBA
- Market and sell your products to consumers
- Identify more products to sell and continue to source, ship, market, and sell more products so that you can scale your business

Once you get the general understanding of how growing your Amazon FBA business works, it becomes a lot easier for you to grow your business. Since the general process of growing and scaling your business ultimately comes down to knowing what your customers want and sourcing more of that product to sell, once you have those steps down, you will be set for success. All you will have to do, then, is continue following the trends and successfully marketing all of your new product listings to your existing audience. With this blueprint in place, you simply follow it over and over again, and in time, your business grows to the level of success that you desire to have with your business.

Create An End-Game Vision

Now that you know what exactly you are planning for, you need to create an end-game vision. Creating an end-game vision gives you the opportunity to have a clear focus for what you are working toward, which is crucial to your success. If you do not have a clear direction and goal for what you want to achieve, you are not going to stay committed because you will have no idea what you are working toward.

Creating your end-game is simple: all you have to do is ask yourself, "if my business were as successful as I desire it to be, what would that look like?" Then, write your answer down and turn this into your goal by making this a SMART goal.

To turn your goal into a SMART goal, identify exactly what you are working toward so that you have something *specific* to focus on. For example, maybe you are working toward having a store that is profitable enough that you can quit your day job and earn your income exclusively from your Amazon FBA business.

Next, you need to make your goal *measurable*. To make your goal measurable, you need to give it some form of specific marker that allows you to know that you have achieved your goal. For example, maybe your goal is to make $5,000 per month or $10,000 per month in your Amazon FBA business so that you can consider it profitable enough for you to quit your day job and live your ideal lifestyle. Having a goal that is measurable helps you know when you are making progress and when you need to adapt your goals so that you can do better in reaching your goals going forward.

Then, you need to make your goal *accurate*. Your goal should be in one way or another relevant to your Amazon FBA business so that you can clearly understand that the two are connected. If your goal is not accurate in that it makes no sense to your

Amazon FBA business, you are going to have a hard time justifying your business because it may seem like a waste of time for you in achieving your goal. Make your goals accurately relevant to your business so that you can clearly understand why the business matters in the first place.

You also need to make your goal *realistic*. If you have a goal that is seemingly outrageous, you are going to have a hard time justifying that it is actually possible for you to achieve that goal. In other words, your goal will intimidate you to the point where you never reach it because you do not believe it is possible. Technically, all things are possible. However, you should choose something that you can truly believe in so that you do not intimidate yourself to the point of quitting before you succeed.

Finally, you need to give yourself a *timeline* for when you are going to achieve your goal by. Although you may not necessarily achieve it by that point, this gives you a set timeline that helps you feel motivated to get into action. If you do not have a timeline associated with your goal it can be easy to say "I will do it later" when in reality, you are not going to get it done at all because you feel like it can be done at any time.

Start At The End

When you are ready to get started in developing your actual action plan for success, you need to start at the end. Start with the SMART goal that you have just made and reverse engineer what steps are necessary for you to achieve this goal. This way, you can clearly identify what is required of you and how you can achieve success with your goal, and you do not miss any steps or build a plan that takes you in the wrong direction.

Another wonderful part of reverse engineering your plan is that you only focus on what is truly necessary, rather than what you think is necessary. This way, you are not adding in extra and unnecessary steps that are going to waste your time rather than get you toward your goal. Reverse engineering goals is a huge opportunity for you to create a direct goal that is going to help you succeed, so always start by working your goals in reverse.

Once you have reverse engineered your goal, look at it going in the right direction from start to finish to ensure that your goal makes sense. This way, you can feel confident that you are working toward success in every step that you take and that nothing is missed *and* nothing is misplaced on your plan chart.

Plan To Have Struggles

Every single plan, no matter how well-crafted, is going to have unexpected bumps and hiccups in it. Even something as simple as planning to take a bath in the evening after work can go awry when you get home and realize that several other things are demanding your time and attention, rendering your schedule full and no time left to bathe. Plans always go off course and struggles will always arise, and accepting that fact early on is a great way to make sure that you are prepared for any struggles that you may face along the way. This is as much about mental preparation as it is about actual practical preparation in your plans.

As you cultivate your plan, make sure that you look at the most likely challenges you are going to face along the way. Identify what those challenges are and pinpoint them on your plan so that you are already aware of what these possible challenges are ahead of time. In many cases, just being aware of the potential for these challenges to arise is plenty for you to avoid them once you hit that point in your plan through preparation and planning.

You should also plan to have enough resources available to navigate any challenges that you may face on your way to success. For example, having extra merchants available and extra funds available is a great way to make sure that if your supplies run out at one merchant, you can get them elsewhere. This also ensures that if you have a cash flow issue in your business early on, you have saved funds to help you deal with that cash flow rather than being left high and dry. This type of planning is important as it helps keep you on track with your success.

Leave The Details For Later

Finally, once you have created the general outline for your plan, you want to make sure that you see this as a guideline. Attempting to plan out every tiny detail that you will engage with from now until you reach your goal is only going to waste a significant amount of your time because you simply cannot know that far in advance. In the end, you will find yourself fixing and revising your details over and over again, which will only leave you feeling like you have wasted a significant amount of your time.

The smartest way to use your plan is to view it as being the guideline that you will follow as you move toward your finish line. This way, you leave room for flexibility, and you are prepared to make adjustments as required while you advance toward your goal. You also do not waste time around your adjustments as you do not have to adjust several tiny little elements of your detailed plan, but rather you can adjust your structure and plan for your details as you go.

When you arrive at each new milestone of your plan, you can go ahead and plan out each detail around that particular milestone to help you move forward. Consider this the short-term part of your plan, as each milestone serves as a goal toward your larger goal. This way, if you find that you need to adjust the details, you are only adjusting a small number of details in your immediate plan, rather than attempting to adjust all of your details.

Another way that this will save you time is through preventing you from having to research everything up front, which can become overwhelming quickly. Instead of researching every little detail, you can go ahead and research only that which is relevant to your immediate goals, allowing you to fully engage with those goals and keep your focus clearly on what needs to be done right now. Once that is done, you can begin researching the next step and outlining your details for that step, allowing you to advance in a way that is not overwhelming and that helps keep you on track with what you are aiming to achieve with your business.

Chapter 3: Why Amazon FBA Is Superior

Now that your mindset is ready and you have a strong idea of how to plan your business, it is time for you to identify why Amazon FBA is likely the best choice for your business. Naturally, if you want to start a business, you want to feel confident that the platform you are going to be starting your business with is the right choice for you. Although I have written this book about starting an Amazon FBA business and want to support you in launching one, it is worth noting that you should do your own research on this topic, too. Below I have outlined why I feel that Amazon FBA is superior to running your own online e-commerce store where you manage and monitor everything on your own. However, you can always do additional research on this topic elsewhere to ensure that you are getting an unbiased, well-rounded opinion on which platform you should be using.

At the end of the day, you are planning on running a business, and you need to take this seriously. Learning how to do the research for yourself and cultivate your own confidence in the platforms that you are using and the decisions that you are making is crucial since this business is entirely your own. If you do not understand why you are making a decision or you are not completely confident in the decision that you are making, you need to slow down and pause before moving forward. After all, you are ultimately the one in charge here!

To help keep this clear and provide you with the full picture, I have given you both why I think Amazon FBA is superior, and what troubles or disadvantages you may face while using Amazon FBA. This way, you can see exactly why this platform is awesome, and where it may not be the best platform out there, giving you an honest view of what to expect. That being said, I do still believe that Amazon FBA is an incredible platform, and the thousands of people making money off of it every single month see it as an incredible platform, too!

Benefits Of Amazon FBA Over Running Your Own Store

First off, I want to address the fact that Amazon FBA is not the only e-commerce platform available to you. However, it is the leading platform for anyone who wants to have their shipments fulfilled by someone other than themselves, which is an advantage that not many other platforms have.

In addition to that, here are some more benefits for you to consider.

International Reach

One of the biggest benefits of using Amazon over running your own online e-commerce store is that Amazon gives you international reach immediately. Although you can reach an international audience with your own platform, the cost of advertising in so many regions would be astronomical. With Amazon FBA, you are automatically presented to an international audience with no additional cost to you because Amazon markets to an international audience.

Having access to an international audience means that as far as sales go, you are capable of reaching a virtually uncapped potential audience. This type of growth is also more cost-effective, meaning that you are not going to have to save or reach certain profit margins in order to begin marketing and selling to your international audience.

Easier Customer Acquisition

Amazon's primary goal is to get more people onto their website to purchase products through their merchants. Whether you sell through FBA or as a standard merchant, Amazon is going to make a percentage of each of your sales, which means that they get paid every time you get paid. For that reason, Amazon wants to drive as many customers to their website as they possibly can so that they are purchasing from their merchants like you.

Since Amazon is doing all of the work of driving clients to their website, all you have to do is market to the customers who land on their website successfully. This way, they shop with your store over any other store being marketed on Amazon, enabling you to have the best sales. If you work with Amazon's advertising features and sponsor advertisements for your products, the process of getting customers onto your product page is virtually effortless and takes very little time and energy on your part to achieve.

Built-In Point Of Sales

Amazon is a ready-made platform, which means everything is already made for you. All you have to do is upload your products to your store, brand your store, and click "go." Amazon's platform will then put together your official product pages and organize your store for you. Everything from the product page to the way it is organized on Amazon's platform to the point of sales features for people to check out with is already made for you, meaning you do not have to do it yourself or hire someone to do it for you.

If you have never built a website before, even using click-and-build website platforms to create your own e-commerce store can be somewhat complicated. There can be a lot for you to do, ranging from choosing which platform to collect payments through and how, and organizing all of the back-end features like when charges are made and how refunds are processed if one is needed. All in all, there is a lot of technical work that goes on with the point of sales alone, never mind the development of product pages and other technical parts of running an e-commerce store. Having everything already made and built-in to your webstore is extremely handy as it saves you the headache of having to learn yourself or the enormous expense of having to hire someone to do it for you.

Amazon Prime Features

As we discussed previously, Amazon Prime is a feature that is available to Amazon FBA store merchants. In fact, as soon as you become an Amazon FBA merchant, you unlock Amazon Prime benefits. With Amazon, they already drive a lot of clients to their website to shop for products on their platform. They also drive a lot *more* to Amazon Prime memberships so that their clients can unlock sweet benefits like Amazon Video, Amazon Music, free 2-day shipping, and other awesome features. The simple reason is that Amazon Prime earns Amazon a significant amount of money on membership fees, and they earn more from Amazon FBA fulfillments, too.

While their driving factor is money, this should be your driving factor, too. Amazon Prime benefits for your customers means that they are far more likely to see your store due to the algorithm *and* that they have an added incentive to buy due to all of the added benefits. At the end of the day, Amazon Prime can be a huge benefit to merchants and customers alike, which can earn you greater sales in the end.

Hassle Free Logistics

Attempting to pick, package, ship, and track all of your orders on your own can be challenging. Massive corporations, like Amazon, have complex systems that they use to ship and track orders every single day, and even still there is the potential for things to get lost or damaged along the way. Could you imagine trying to replicate their complex systems on your own? It would not be feasible. For starters, this would put a lot of stress on your shoulders to have to get to the shipping facilities on a regular basis to get products out to your customers. It would also mean that you are held liable for your own mistakes, which are inevitable when you are managing so many shipments and can be costly if you shoulder that liability yourself. Furthermore, this is simply not scalable if you want to grow your business unless you want to practically live at the shipping plant where you can send products out on a constant basis. And hiring someone to help you? Not worth the investment.

Amazon FBA offers hassle-free logistics by dealing with virtually everything relating to inventory. As you know, they are responsible for receiving your products from your merchant, organizing your products, picking and packaging them for orders, shipping them, tracking them, and dealing with everything around returns or exchanges. This takes a lot off of your own shoulders *and* makes them liable for any mishaps that take place during the shipping process.

Disadvantages Of Amazon FBA

Although Amazon FBA is an amazing platform with plenty of wonderful features, there are definitely things to consider as far as disadvantages go. Amazon FBA can have drawbacks that make the platform somewhat challenging to navigate, or that perhaps make it take longer for newcomers to learn how to use the platform efficiently. Recognizing these disadvantages in advance can help you determine if you are willing to deal with these disadvantages. It can also help you prepare and plan for them so that they do not pose a significant risk for you in the future by making you an informed business owner.

Difficult To Track Inventory

First things first, it can be somewhat difficult to track and manage inventory with Amazon FBA if you are not aware of how to use the system. Although Amazon does their best to keep everything updated and organized through their own tracking system, if you are not creating your own tracking system it can be a hassle to know what needs to be ordered and when.

The best way to navigate this disadvantage is to set up a system for you to manage and monitor your products on a consistent basis. This way, when your products are in need of being ordered again, you know what needs to be ordered, when, and how many. Remember, at the end of the day, Amazon's systems are for *Amazon*. They use their tracking and inventory management systems as a tool to help their fulfillment employees find the products that they need to fulfill orders. You are going to need to come up with your own way of tracking and managing inventory so that you can fulfill your own needs, such as keeping popular items in stock and ordering new products.

Potential Increase In Returns

Amazon FBA offers an easy returns policy so that if your client does not like what they have ordered, they can easily return it for a refund. When you run your own Amazon shop, you are able to choose your return policies and, generally, it is more challenging to facilitate returns anyway because you are using smaller, private shipping companies. This means that returns are generally not facilitated because people are not interested in dealing with the more complex return policy that smaller merchants offer. With Amazon FBA, however, the easy return is a part of their Amazon Prime feature, and more people tend to use it due to how easy it is.

This increase in ease could mean an increase in product returns, particularly if you are selling products that are low in quality or that are inaccurately described on your platform. This means that you could have a harder time selling out of products and maintaining your sales if you are not careful. The best way to mitigate this risk is to ensure that you are always checking for quality and selling high-quality products to your customers and that the descriptions are accurate. This way, you are less likely to get returns.

Additional Expenses And Fees

All of the added benefits of Amazon FBA certainly does come with increased fees and expenses. As we discussed previously, there are certain fee structures and schedules that you are going to have to work with in order to use this platform to run your business. Of course, for many people, all of the added convenience is well worth the investment, especially since you are likely still going to come out profitable in the end anyway. Although it may cut into your profits some, it may turn out to be cheaper in the long run due to you not having to spend so much on your own inventory storage and shipping fees.

Another way that this can be seen as a benefit is that you are only paying expenses to one company, Amazon, rather than multiple companies between shipping, storing, packaging materials, and otherwise. In the end, it can be a lot easier for you to track and may turn out to be a lot cheaper as well. For that reason, this expense is often seen as both a disadvantage and a blessing for merchants since it does exist, but it also comes with plenty of positive benefits.

Difficult Shipping Prep

Until you learn how, navigating the shipping process of getting your products from your supplier to the Amazon FBA warehouse facilities can be fairly challenging. First, you need to discover which facility you are to ship your products so that you can get your products there in the first place. This way, you can give your supplier the right information to get your products to the Amazon FBA facilities. Then, you also have to make sure that your products are compliant and that they are registered with Amazon to be received. If your products are not compliant and if they have the wrong identification codes on them, Amazon will deny the shipment and send it back to your supplier. This can lead to a costly and lengthy process of getting your products sent back to Amazon again with the proper product codes registered this time.

The first few times you go through the process can be challenging, which can make this probably one of the more difficult learning curves of having an Amazon FBA store to begin with. Once you navigate this process a few times, however, you will find that it becomes easier. All you have to be extra cautious about is product codes, to avoid having shipments denied by Amazon when they reach the facility.

Greater Competition

Amazon does do a great deal of work to drive customers to their website, but it doesn't mean that they are driving their customers to *your* shop. Unless, of course, your shop is relevant and has a high positive rating with your clients, in which case Amazon will rank you higher in their algorithm. At the end of the day, Amazon wants to get their customers into the best merchants' shops so that they can purchase great products and have a positive experience. This is what will provide Amazon with return customers, which in turn provides their merchants like you with return customers. Naturally, you are going to be driving customers to your shop too through your own efforts, but this is generally how it works on Amazon.

Because of this, it can be challenging to get everyone to land on your store instead of the store of your competition. Your competitors are all fighting for the same sales that you are fighting for, which means that it can take a lot of work to get people to choose your store over someone else's. Especially at first prior to having any reputation built, this can be a difficult part of the process to navigate.

The best way to offset this disadvantage is to build a strong brand and brand reputation while making brand recognition a priority for you. This can all be done by taking your marketing into your own hands and making a name for yourself while also driving your audience directly to your own store. This way, people know who you are and are more likely to trust you over other merchants on Amazon, meaning you are more likely to get the sales.

Possible Reduced Perceived Value

Although this tends to vary from store to store, some people believe that products that are sold and shipped on Amazon are lower quality than products sold elsewhere. If you are attempting to target an audience that prefers smaller, local shopping type experiences, you might have a hard time getting your audience into your shop in the first place because they may see you as being poor quality.

This lower perceived value that tends to come along with Amazon's reputation often comes from the fact that there are many merchants selling counterfeit products or knock-offs, as well as many who source low-quality products from cheap overseas suppliers. Although you can certainly source from cheaper overseas suppliers, it is up to you as the merchant to make sure that the products you are getting are still valuable enough to be purchased and kept by your audience. If you are not being cautious about this, you might find yourself having a lot of returns and losing your own reputation right from the jump by being a low quality, careless merchant on Amazon.

The best way to offset this disadvantage is to build a brand for yourself and set yourself apart from day one. Make sure that you put effort into having quality products, and make sure that your customers see this effort being made so that they know that you are taking pride in your store. This way, they are going to see that you have a high-quality store and, because of that, they will trust in your store and likely choose your products over anyone else's.

Chapter 4: Getting Started With Amazon FBA

It's time! You are now fully aware of what you are getting into, have a strong idea of how you can prepare for your store and are equipped with the mindset of a winner! If you have come this far and you are still feeling confident that Amazon FBA is right for you, then you are ready to get started with building your shop and earning profits from the Amazon FBA platform!

As promised, this book is step by step, so we are going to get started with the very basic first step: opening your account and getting it set up for you to run your shop.

What To Know Before You Start

Before you start setting up your account, it is important that you know what account options are available to you. When you set up your account, you are going to notice that you are invited to start either an "individual" account or a "professional" account. If you want to have a business where you can scale it and use Amazon FBA, you have to sign up for a professional account. This account comes with a $39.99 monthly fee as of 2019, and this provides you with all of the benefits of the Amazon platform, including having your own storefront for people to purchase through.

If you choose to open up a free individual account, you are not going to have all of the benefits of being able to scale your business or use Amazon FBA's features. Although you will be able to sell on Amazon on your own, you will not be able to access the features that you need to run an FBA account. For that reason, you should not go this route when you set up your account unless you plan on running a small hobby shop all on your own.

Setting Up Your Account

When you are ready to get started, you can open your Amazon FBA account by going to the Amazon website and scrolling to the bottom of their page and selecting the button that says "Make Money With Us."

Upon selecting that feature, you are going to be walked through a step-by-step process of starting your Amazon FBA account. This will begin with some basic information, such as inputting your email address, choosing a password, and filling in some basic information about what type of shop you want to open and what products you are going to be selling on your shop.

This part of the process is incredibly straightforward and is perhaps the easiest part of the entire process. You will find that Amazon makes it easy by giving you a step by step tutorial the entire way that ensures that you fill in all of the right information to the best of your ability.

Chapter 5: Choosing Your Products

With your Amazon FBA account open and organized, the next step you have to work on is choosing your products and establishing your brand. Your brand should be established around your products so that it makes sense, which is why we are going to focus on how you can choose your products first.

Because you are opening up a shop as a retail merchant, the products that you choose to sell are the difference between success and failure with this business model. If you choose the wrong products, you will either struggle to sell them, or you will fail to make a single profit off of them in the long run. In fact, you may even find yourself paying more on those products than you are making in return, resulting in you actually losing money through this business model.

Fortunately, mishaps like that only happen if you fail to do your research and have no idea what you are looking for. Since you are here reading this book, you are going to gain insight into everything you need to know about product sourcing to avoid paying the price in the end.

In this chapter, we are going to walk through the process of choosing what products you are going to sell and finding a place to source them from. We are also going to discuss important considerations about customization features, which is an option that has the capacity to make your product sales higher than anyone else's. Finally, we will discuss important things that you need to consider about regarding how your products are going to be transported to the Amazon warehouse.

Deciding On Your Product Category

The first thing you have to do before you start picking specific products to sell on Amazon is to decide what category you want to sell products in. Amazon offers tons of different categories for you to sell in, plenty of which are massively successful and offer excellent potential for your business to thrive. For that reason, you are going to have to pick a category for yourself based on what interests you and what you want to cultivate a brand in!

When picking a category, there are a few things that you are going to want to consider. Naturally, not *every* category is going to offer growth potential and massive profitability, so you are going to want to consider growth and profit potential for your ideal category. You can do this by simply searching up the trends of your ideal category on your favorite search engine and seeing how each industry is performing overall in the e-commerce world. This way, you can get a good feel for what offers growth and what does not.

You also need to consider what category you are going to be most interested in working with long term. Even if you are planning on building a completely hands-off store that is mostly passive, you are still going to want to have a store that sells products that you are interested in. This way, you have an easier time talking about your products and promoting your store early on, offering you the greatest chance of getting people to look at your products in the first place. If you attempt to market your store and you are selling products that you do not care about or that you are not knowledgeable in, you are going to have a hard time getting anyone to listen.

In fact, not knowing much about your products or industry can be a bigger problem than just marketing difficulties. Not knowing about what you are selling can result in you not knowing what to look for when it comes to finding high-quality items which, in the long run, can completely diminish the success of your store. You should have at least a basic understanding of what you are selling so that you are able to offer products that are of high quality.

If you have no idea where to start with finding the right category that meets these qualifications, Amazon's website is a great spot! A great way to research their most popular categories is to simply go to their website and see what exists on their main page. All of their most popular categories and products will be featured here for their audience to see. Searching this page can give you a great idea for what is popular and what people are looking for so that you can pick a category that both interests you and attracts a high audience every single month.

Choosing Exact Products to Sell

Once you have an idea of what category you want to sell in, you need to choose exactly what products you want to stock in your store. Upon opening your store, ideally, you want to have 5-10 products available for your customers to purchase so that they have plenty to choose from. Choosing each product is going to follow the same procedure as the one outlined below, so repeat this process a few times over until you have 5-10 products chosen for your store.

The first step in choosing a product to sell is narrowing your products down to which ones are going to actually fit within your category. Then, you need to identify which products are the most popular in your category to ensure that there is a strong enough demand for the product that you are ultimately going to choose to sell. At this point, you should note the top 10-15 products in your chosen category so that you have a strong idea of what products are performing well. Through this, you will see both the exact products that are performing well *and* the trends that exist in the top performers so that you know what specifications to look for with your own products.

With a healthy number of popular products on your radar, you now need to start narrowing those products down to find out what is going to be your best option for selling. There are a few things that you are going to want to look for to qualify products for being worthy of your investment when it comes to selling them.

First, you want to see how people are responding to those products. You can start by searching for each product on Amazon and getting an idea of what the overall reviews are and whether or not people are actually liking the product upon purchasing it.

Look over multiple listings to ensure that you get a well-rounded vision of whether or not the product is actually desirable by the people shopping for it.

Next, you want to look at the content of those reviews. Pay attention to what people are saying, especially when they are saying something that critiques the product. If you find that people wish that the product had different features or options or that it came in different colors or styles, note that down. If you find that multiple people are complaining about something in common, write that down. Pay close attention to opportunities for you to improve on the product in your own shop so that you have a competitive advantage over the people who are already selling the same product on Amazon. This way, you can accentuate these competitive edges in your product listing, giving you the opportunity to fill the product gap that other merchants have made so far.

A final element of the reviews that you want to pay attention to is the number of reviews that each product is receiving. If you look at a product and there are hundreds of reviews on each product, assume that that part of the market is already covered and that you are not going to have a strong competitive advantage coming in late to the game. Unlike those other listings, you do not have a strong seller reputation, any credibility ratings, or anything else helping you achieve success in your store. Instead of trying to compete with people who are already killing it, look for products that have around 30-50 reviews. If Amazon's top-selling product on a listing search retrieves you 30-50 reviews, you can feel confident that you have found a popular product that does not presently exist in a saturated market. This means that you have a *much* higher chance of achieving strong sales with this product than you would if you tried to dive into a saturated market.

Beyond reviews, there are also some great platforms that you can use to help you identify what products are a good selling opportunity. JungleScout, for example, is a platform that you can use that will help you qualify products by giving you important statistics on them that are pulled directly from Amazon's website. Through this platform, you can find how products rank, what their trends are, and whether or not they are likely to turn a good profit. This is a great way to look even deeper into the specifics of your product so that you can find the best products to sell.

Finally, before you add any product to your shop, you should always test that product yourself. Look for a product on Amazon that would be a direct competitor for the product that you want to sell and order a unit. Give the product a try and get a hands-on experience for whether or not you actually like the product and whether or not it is worth the investment. This is a great opportunity for you to see what the quality of the product is like, whether or not you can actually stand behind it, and if people are going to be likely to purchase it. As well, you can determine for yourself what features you would like to see on your own units to make them higher quality and more worth the investment, offering you a chance to customize your competitive edge in a powerful way.

The last part of choosing products for you to sell in your shop is determining what the profitability on each product is going to be. You can do this by identifying possible sources for the product using the guide below and then looking on Amazon to see what competitive units will be sold for. Ensure that you are factoring prices modestly, as even a superior unit will not sell for much higher than the market average for products in your chosen category. This will help you determine a truer profit margin for what you are most likely going to receive once you purchase and begin selling the product yourself.

In general, most people aim to have a profit margin that is going to be 30% or higher, with most merchants preferring a profit margin of 50% or higher. This ensures that you are going to earn a high enough profit on your products that you can scale your business *and* keep some of the profits for yourself. In this case, you would invest back your principal plus 15-25%, and save 15-25% as being your personal income from your profits.

Sourcing Your Products

Sourcing products for your Amazon store is actually incredibly simple. Although there are plenty of ways to do this, the most common way to do it that will save you plenty of money is through Alibaba. Alibaba is somewhat like an Amazon platform for wholesalers and suppliers to sell their products to retailers that sell in both e-commerce and brick and mortar alike. On the platform, you search for the product that you want to sell and find a supplier that you are going to shop through to fill your Amazon store.

Finding a supplier on Alibaba is simple because it gives you access to thousands of suppliers who all have various options for you to purchase from their shop to fill yours. You also gain the opportunity to compare merchants to find the ones that are going to give you the best deals and the highest quality products based on what budget you are going into your shop with. Although there are other ways to find merchants, this tends to be easiest as most suppliers have low-quality websites that can be rather challenging to navigate. Alibaba, however, offers everything in an organized, easy-to-navigate manner that makes shopping for products effortless.

When it comes to choosing what supplier you are going to go with, there are various factors that you need to consider to ensure that you are getting the best deal possible. Below I am going to give you details on what to look for to help you pick the best supplier that is going to be reliable and offer the highest quality of products to your shop. This way, you know exactly what to look for, and you can shop from Alibaba with confidence.

The first thing you want to do when searching for a supplier on Alibaba is to search for one who can provide you with exactly what you are looking for. Naturally, if a supplier cannot give you exactly what you need, this means they are likely not going to be the supplier that you want to work with. Narrow down your search by finding suppliers that sell exactly what you are looking for, right down to the specific customizations that you require for your product.

Another great idea when it comes to sourcing products on Alibaba is to search for where your chosen product is actually produced, and not just areas where it is being sold. If you can research and identify where the product is actually being produced, then you can narrow down the scope of your search to only provide you with suppliers located in that region. It is likely that any suppliers located outside of that region will be middlemen and will charge more because they are purchasing products from suppliers and then selling them again for an additional profit.

Once you have suppliers that match the above criteria, you can begin to scan each supplier for quality. You want to make sure that you are choosing a supplier who consistently provides higher quality products so that you do not run into issues later when you are selling the products to your own customers. You can qualify suppliers by looking at their other products and getting a feel for what they sell overall. Ideally, the supplier you buy should be specializing in your industry, not blending together several different industries in what they produce. For example, if you are looking for apparel items and find that your supplier also produces tech gear and hardware, chances are they are not providing high-quality items. Your chosen supplier should only be producing products for your industry as this proves that they are focused on doing well in that industry and, therefore, their products are likely much higher quality.

In addition to paying attention to make sure that they are staying loyal to the right industry, also carefully read through the descriptions of their products. Professional companies will give great detail about their products so that you are clear about what you are buying and receiving from their company. Unprofessional companies that are going to be harder to work with and that will likely have lower quality products tend to give vague details about their products or will provide details that are seemingly irrelevant about the product itself because they are trying to make a sale.

Another important part of working together with suppliers on Alibaba is communication and correspondence. Unlike shopping for yourself where you simply choose what you want, pay, and have it shipped, suppliers are going to be someone that you communicate on a fairly regular basis. When you work with a supplier to supply your business, you should feel confident about the correspondence that you share. Look for suppliers who are easy to communicate with by sending them some questions about their products and about how the process works when you are working with them. Then, pay attention to the responses that they give you. A professional company will respond clearly and directly to your questions in a way that is easy to understand. Unprofessional companies will provide strange responses, will not directly answer your questions, or will make it clear that they are more focused on the sale than providing quality service and products to you. Avoid the ones who respond unprofessionally.

When you choose what questions to ask your suppliers, make sure that you are asking ones that actually determine whether or not they are qualified. Ask them questions such as how long they have been in business for, what their process is like, how they check for quality and other questions that are going to qualify them as your supplier. As you begin to receive answers to these questions back, you will be able to compare them, and it will become incredibly obvious about who is knowledgeable and providing high-quality services and who is not.

Finally, pay attention to some of the ratings available around each seller. Each supplier on Alibaba will have ratings and reviews left by other people who have purchased through them. Although these are not the primary deciding factor, getting a general idea of other people's experiences with that supplier can help you determine if it is worth it or not to do business with that person. If you find that you are seeing a lot of bad reviews or a lot of common complaints about issues that seem to go unrectified, it may be a good idea to steer clear of that particular supplier.

The next thing you want to do is check if the product is available for private label. Private label products are products that will be produced by a supplier and then marketed with your branding on them. If you are looking to expand your business through Amazon FBA, cultivating your own brand and putting that brand everywhere, including on your products, is an excellent way to develop brand recognition. This is key in helping you stand apart from the rest of the crowd, so do not overlook this part of the process!

Finally, you need to consider your suppliers against your own logistics. You want to choose a supplier who is going to offer you the best value for your investment, so find someone who offers the best price per unit. You should also look for the supplier that is going to offer the best shipping fees to ensure that you are getting a good deal there. As well, if you think you are going to want to expand out, make sure you choose a supplier who has products that you are going to be interested in supplying so that you can continue using the same supplier going forward. This will keep your paperwork more efficient and will make it easier for you to determine which products to add since you already feel confident in that supplier.

The last thing to do after qualifying a supplier and before purchasing your units is to request a sample product. To do this, simply ask your supplier, and often, they will provide you with a discounted unit for you to sample to make sure that the product is going to be something that you want to sell to your customers. Again, it is always important that you sample products so that you can feel confident that you are going to be selling high-quality products. Skipping this step could result in low-quality units being purchased in high quantities and then sitting in Amazon's warehouse, costing you money because no one wants to buy them or they keep getting returned. Mistakes like this can be costly in the end, so avoid them by quality checking your own products every single time.

Offering Customization Features

When it comes to really setting yourself apart on Amazon, having customizable features on your units is a great way. When people are shopping, they like to feel like they are more in control over their experience. They want to have the opportunity to choose things such as whether they want the base product, the intermediate product, or the advanced product. They want to choose the color or the design, and the style of the product to ensure that it fits into their lives. Offering choices to your audience is a great way to stand apart from the rest of the merchants on Amazon as you give your customers a wider range of choices.

The key when it comes to offering choices is to make sure that you are not offering *too* many, and that the ones you are offering are ones that people would actually be interested in purchasing. Ensuring that you pay attention to these two key parts of offering customizations will help you get the most sales in your shop.

The reason why you want to refrain from offering too many choices is that too many choices can overwhelm people. Studies have shown that if they have too many items to choose from, a person will generally choose nothing because they become intimidated by the decision, and they struggle to commit to any one thing. A great example of this happening is when you see people in line at a fast food restaurant taking several minutes to pick an item, only to find themselves ordering the exact same thing every time. The reason why this happens is that their brain goes into overdrive trying to weigh all of the pros and cons of each item before finally settling on one thing. The same will happen if you offer too many solutions in your store. Offering customizations without going overboard on the number of customizations available is key for helping people have more to choose from without making it too difficult of a decision.

For the customization features you do choose, it is important that you choose ones that are actually going to be popular. You want to offer designs or colors that people are going to be interested in and that are actually going to sell out. A great way to find out which colors are most popular is to search the top listings and see which ones are selling out the most. This way, you are able to get a clear idea for what colors are most desirable by your customers. Do your best to always stock all of the most popular colors so that your shop has all of the desirable customization features that people are looking for, as this will give you a competitive edge. Now, rather than having to search through multiple listings to find color options they like, they can just search through yours!

Transporting Your Products to Amazon

Once you have found all of the products you want, including the customization features, you have to get your products transported to Amazon. On Alibaba, transporting items to Amazon is fairly simple as you will just input your Amazon shipping address into the shipping destination when you are checking out. You can find your Amazon shipping address on your Amazon FBA account.

Before you purchase your products and finalize the shipping arrangements, make sure that you get the UPC codes, or the product codes, and input them into your Amazon product list. If you do not get these accurate numbers and upload them into your Amazon account, your products **will** be denied by Amazon, and you will have to pay the shipping fee all over again to get them transported back there. This can be costly, so <u>do not miss this step</u>.

You can upload products by creating a shipping plan on your Amazon FBA account. To do this, you will go to your account and select "Upload Shipping Plan." Then, you will provide Amazon with a spreadsheet that provides directions for how the template should be used.

You will also need to create five additional sections on your template:

- Data definitions, which are the definitions at the top of each column which describes what you are listing in that column
- Plan example, which provides an example for shipping individual products
- Plan template, which is a blank spreadsheet provided for shipping individual products
- Case quantity example, which provides examples for shipping products that are packed in cases
- Case quantity template, which is a blank spreadsheet provided for shipping case-packed products

This shipping plan actually has a template already made for it on your Amazon FBA account which will help you get started. The template is outlined with clear instructions on where you should be placing information on it, so all you have to do is fill it out with your own information and then upload it into Amazon's database. This makes uploading your files incredibly simple as you can guarantee that they are going to be done right every single time. This way, if you do not have any experience with spreadsheets and shipments, you will have an easy time figuring it out.

Once this spreadsheet has been finalized and approved, all you have to do is purchase your products and have them shipped according to your shipping plan! At this point, it should be as simple as purchasing them and having them shipped. However, you might want to communicate with your chosen supplier to inform them of your shipping plans so that they are also aware of what needs to happen in order for Amazon to receive the products.

Chapter 6: Creating Your Brand

While your first products are on their way to Amazon, it is a good idea for you to begin creating your brand. As you already know, your brand is key in helping you set yourself apart from other brands that already exist on Amazon. With your brand, you can create familiarity on Amazon itself, as well as on other platforms such as Instagram, Facebook, and Twitter, where you can drive traffic directly to your Amazon store.

If you chose to create private label products, you would want to have your brand already established *before* ordering them so that they are privately labeled with the right branding. For that reason, you should do this step before you officially purchase your products so that you can feel confident that they are going to match your branding.

In this chapter, we are going to explore all of the basics of launching a brand for your Amazon account, including how you can use other platforms to drive traffic to your website. You will also learn about how you can protect your brand to avoid having other Amazon merchants rip your brand off and potentially destroy your reputation and the credibility of your business along the way.

Choose Your Brand Identity

First things first, you need to choose your brand identity. Your brand identity is the identity by which you are going to be recognized, so you need to make sure that you choose one that is attractive and coherent. Your brand identity includes your name, your logo, your font, your colors, and your imagery. All of these factors are relevant in cultivating your brand, so make sure that you pay attention to all of them.

The name of your brand should be something relevant and catchy. It should make sense to your brand so that it is clear as to why you have chosen this name and what it represents. Ideally, your brand name should not be your own name, unless your own name is already popular and well known. Instead, choose a one or two-word brand name that represents what you are selling so that people will immediately recognize it and know who you are once you begin to establish brand familiarity.

Your logo and brand fonts should be the same, as you want to use your brand fonts in your logo. Typically, brands will choose two fonts that they are going to use to represent their brand. The first font is generally the header font that they are using, and the second font is the body font. These two fonts should go nicely together and should have a feel that is relevant to your industry. For example, if you are selling professional office products, you should use clean fonts like Arial or Helvetica. If you are in an elegant industry, choose something like a script header and a simple body font, such as Dancing Script and Arial.

You need to choose a few colors that are also going to represent your brand. Ideally, you should have three to four colors for your brand: one or two primary colors and then two secondary colors. Your colors are going to be used on everything from your labels to your graphics and everywhere else, so make sure they go well together and that they fit into your overall image. They should also be relevant to your industry by providing the right look and feel to your brand, as out-of-place colors can quickly make your brand seem unprofessional or misplaced.

Finally, you want to choose the actual imagery of your brand. Most brands will produce what is called a mood board, which is essentially a collection of graphics that give the feel for what your brand is going to offer. You might have people lying at the beach and sunsets if your brand is for lounging and relaxing, or you might have pictures of minimalism and fresh flowers if you want a minimalist eco-friendly appearance. Create whatever mood board you desire based on the look and feel that you want your brand to have.

Once you have put all of this together, lay it all next to each other to get a feel for what your final brand is going to be. This will give you an idea as to whether or not it works together and if it is going to provide the right look for your company. If you find that it does not perfectly reflect your brand, you are going to want to make a few adjustments to it so that it gives a better and more coherent feel for your customers.

Apply For Brand Registry

After you have created your brand, go on Amazon, and apply for a brand registry. You should do this before you do anything else with your brand as this is going to protect your brand from possible identity theft on Amazon. A brand registry can be applied for by going onto your professional seller account, heading to your settings, and selecting the "Brand Registry" feature.

In order to register your brand, you are going to have to provide the following information to Amazon:

- The name of your brand (it will need to be registered with U.S. Patent and Trademarks first)
- Brand serial number from your USPTO
- The countries where your products are manufactured and distributed by
- Image of your brand name on a product that you will be selling
- Image of your product label
- Image of your product

Although this can take some time, it is worth doing so that you can protect your brand from being stolen by anyone else on Amazon. Remember, Amazon is an international marketplace, so having this added layer of protection is crucial in helping you avoid any unwanted brand identity theft that could take place.

As well, having this brand registration unlocks more branded features for you on Amazon, including the ability to brand your own storefront and product pages as per your brand's appearance. It is well worth the investment!

Brand Your Product Pages

Each time you upload products to your shop, you should be branding those pages. There are three areas of your product page that you want to brand in order to have your brand clearly displayed for your customers to see.

The first part of your product page you want to brand is your title. Your title can have up to 200 characters in it, so do your best to create a full title that features your brand's name, the title of the product, and anything else that someone may search when they are looking for your products.

The second part of your product page that you should brand is your product description. On Amazon's product pages, you can include up to 5 bullet points of information, with each bullet point containing up to 255 characters. Use these bullet points to provide clear information about what benefits people will gain from using the products and any search terms that they may be looking for when they are searching for products like yours. Refrain from making the bullet points spammy by listing search terms without any context, as this may actually reduce your rankings on Amazon's SEO, or search engine returns.

Finally, you want to brand your pictures. Your pictures should clearly display your product with your branded private label. You can also watermark your images with your brand name in the corner or somewhere along the edges, where it will not interrupt your image so that you can brand your product there as well. Each of your pictures should be relevant to your brand by having your brand's color scheme and mood artistically weaved into your picture. For example, if you have a fresh and clean eco-brand, you might photograph your product on a white background next to fresh green plants. If you have a rustic western brand, you might photograph your product on a wood background next to something like a vintage piece of furniture or decoration. Avoid going too crazy with your images; however, as cluttered images or images with too many decorations in them can be distracting and confusing. People may get overwhelmed with what they are looking at and may find themselves looking elsewhere instead of looking at your products because they simply do not know what they are looking at.

Brand Your Product Labels

In addition to branding your store, you also want to brand your product labels. Whenever you can, source products that allow for private labels so that you can label your products with your logo, fonts, and color scheme. Doing so is going to help you create products that are marketing your brand for you as they feature all of this information directly on them. Now, when someone buys your product, they are going to remember the brand it was purchased from, and they can use this information to buy more for themselves or to encourage their friends to buy something from you.

When you brand your product labels, try to stick to generally the same look on all products. Having the same background colors, imagery, and general design on your product labels will ensure that you are keeping your look uniform. This way, you are increasing your chances of having brand recognition because you are producing the same look every time. A great example of this is Coca-Cola. Their brand is represented by an iconic red with their scripted logo. Every time you look at a Coca-Cola product, you immediately know what it is because the branding is uniform and clear every single time.

Brand Your Amazon Storefront

On Amazon, after you register your brand, you are going to have the opportunity to brand your storefront. Your storefront is basically like your webstore or your own private webpage on Amazon's platform that displays your products for sale. Branding your storefront is an important part of making it memorable so that people want to see it and pay attention to your products when they land on your page.

You can brand your storefront by choosing how many pages you are going to have displayed on your store, what those pages are, and what categories they revolve around. You want to design your pages and categories in a way that reinforces the image and brand that you have already begun to develop so that when people land on your page, it feels like it truly belongs to your brand. In other words, *it makes sense.*

When you develop your storefront, a branded video on your front page that is about 30 seconds long is actually an incredible way for you to boost your viewership and your recognition. Although this will take more effort and time investment on your end, doing it can have a huge impact on your customers and can support you with increasing your sales numbers.

With your branded storefront, you can choose to have your own URL if you desire so that you can market both on Amazon's platform and off of it. If you really want to set yourself apart from the other brands on Amazon, this is a great feature. However, it is not necessary, so do not feel like you have to do this if you do not want to. You can still make plenty of money with your Amazon FBA platform without your own URL.

Brand Your Amazon Ads

We will go deeper into advertising with Amazon in Chapter 7. However, it is important for you to know that this is a feature that is available to help you brand your business. Amazon offers three types of ads: sponsored product ads, sponsored brand ads, and sponsored display ads. Taking advantage of sponsored brand ads is a great way to promote your brand and help boost brand recognition so that you are more likely to make sales with your brand on Amazon. As well, sponsored brand ads provide you with the opportunity to show people what your brand is so that they can find your store and discover what products they are interested in, rather than having your individual products being marketed to them.

Brand Your Other Platforms

Once your Amazon brand has been built, brand your other platforms, too. With Amazon, you are not required to use social media to drive traffic to your store. However, it does help. Driving your own traffic to your own store by building a brand on social media and using that brand to funnel people increases your sales because it means you are no longer relying solely on Amazon's algorithm. You certainly do not have to do this, and if you do not want much involvement in this business you should skip this step, but if you really want to grow your store, this is an important step.

If you are on Instagram, Facebook, Twitter, or anywhere else on social media or the internet itself, make sure that you are branding your accounts. Use your logo in your graphics, choose graphics that are relevant to your brand, and create a brand that is going to help you establish recognition. Then, encourage people from your brand to find their way to your platform and purchase your products!

There are plenty of great books about branding on social media, so I highly recommend you grab one and use that as a part of your mindset growth and personal development if this is something you want to do. A book that is specifically designed around this topic will provide you with ample advice on how to brand each account and how to post in a way that accentuates your brand and gets your name out there in a bigger way.

Chapter 7: Launching Products With Amazon

With everything in place and your products arriving at Amazon's warehouse, it is time for you to launch your products! Launching products on Amazon is actually incredibly simple, but it does take some practice to memorize each of the steps and have a big impact on each launch. As well, you will find that each launch grows as you go because you are better at it each time, and you already have some credibility established around your brand and your reputation. The momentum between your own knowledge and this recognition will help each launch do better than the last, so long as you grow with the momentum.

In this chapter, we are going to go through a simple launch sequence so that you know exactly what you need to be doing in order to succeed with your brand. As you launch your first products, follow this sequence exactly so that you are able to get everything done. Make a note of anything you feel you could do differently to accentuate your strengths and do better, though, so that you can create your own launch sequence that perfectly fits your business and keeps you growing.

Optimizing Your Listings

The first thing you need to do to launch your product on Amazon is to optimize your listing. Once your listing is branded as per the instructions in Chapter 6, all you have to do is upload Search Engine Optimization (SEO) features into your listing. Since Amazon works like a search engine, just like Google search does, using SEO is important. This will help your listings show up toward the top of the page, meaning you are more likely to get viewed over the people who fall later than you in the listing rankings.

The best way to SEO your product page is to use relevant search terms in your title and your product description, without going overboard or being spammy about it. Amazon actually has a clause built into their algorithm that prevents people from ranking well if they put too many keywords in their listing. Amazon assumes that these listings are spam and then ranks them incredibly low, preventing them from ever getting found by anyone who is using Amazon to shop. The key is to use keywords sparingly, and in a way that actually makes sense in the flow of your listing.

A great way to spot rich keywords that you could use for your listing is to use a keyword search tool such as Keyword.io or Google's built-in keyword app. Both of these will give you the opportunity to search for keywords that are relevant to your industry so that you can use the best keywords on your listing. Each keyword tool will have its own way of ranking the quality of keywords, so make sure that you follow this ranking to find keywords that are going to be supportive in helping you get found. Typically, these ranking tools will help you avoid keywords that are saturated or ones that are not used enough to really be worth the effort of fitting them into your description.

It is also important that you do not overuse a single keyword in your description. Using a keyword any more than 1-2% of your total description can result in you being marked as spam and your posts not being shown. Find ways to use relevant keywords without overusing them by choosing alternative words, too, so that you can stay optimized in the search parameters.

Outlining Your Launch Strategy

Once your product listings are all set up and optimized, and your store is ready to go, you can outline your launch strategy. It is crucial that you do not start a launch plan until after your entire shop is set up and ready to go, as doing so could result in you not having everything ready come your chosen launch date. Pushing back launches to accommodate tech glitches or malfunctions is incredibly unprofessional and can massively destroy the momentum of your launch, so avoid that by preparing everything first.

With everything prepared, you can go ahead and create a schedule that will outline your strategy. Ideally, your schedule should include the date that you want your shop ready by, the date that you will start organic advertising, the dates that you will start paid advertising (and what types of paid advertising will be started when) and the dates that you will monitor your growth for important metrics in how you can improve momentum. Having all of this outlined in your schedule in advance will ensure that you know exactly what needs to be done on every day leading up to the official launch of your product so that you can stay on track and continue building momentum.

As you will quickly learn, momentum is the backbone of any strong launch, so having a strong flow of momentum building up around your products and business is essential. You want to build up momentum around your launch, as well as use that building momentum from each product to carry into your next product launch so that you can get ahead each time.

Note that when you launch your first products, you are also going to be launching your store for the first time. For that reason, you should use all of these strategies for the items that you think are going to be most popular, *and* for your branded store in general. This way, you are promoting both your store and brand itself and the products that you are going to have for sale. This will build momentum and recognition around both your brand and your products, making for a much more successful launch right from the jump. In future launches, you will not have to do as much work around promoting your brand to really get your name out there.

Launching Your Advertisements

As I mentioned previously, Amazon has three different types of advertisements: sponsored product ads, sponsored brand ads, and sponsored display ads. You are going to want to make use of sponsored product ads and sponsored brand ads at the very least, but ideally, you should use all three to really get your name out there and make the biggest impact in your launch.

Below, I will discuss how all three of these ads work and what you need to do to configure them for your launch.

Sponsored Product Ads

Sponsored product ads are the advertisements that are featured at the top of search listings when a customer searches for a product that they want. This type of ad is excellent to launch after you have officially launched your product on your store, as it will help your product appear over anyone else's in search rankings.

You can make a sponsored product ad on Amazon by choosing which product you want to sponsor and following the step-by-step process of designing your ad. Ideally, you should sponsor the products that you think will be most popular so that your money is spent well on these advertisements.

When it comes to creating sponsored product ads, you will go to the product you want to sponsor and tap "sponsor product." Then, you are going to set your target in terms of who your purchasing audience is so that Amazon shows your ad to the right people. You can find out who your target audience is easily by looking at your industry as a whole to get a feel for who is a part of it, and by looking at existing products in other people's store to get a feel for who their audience is. Set your parameters around your findings.

Once your target is organized, you can choose your budget, or how much you want to spend on your ad. Naturally, the more you spend, the more you are going to get seen. However, avoid spending more than you can reasonably budget for so that you are not wasting your money. Ideally, your sponsored product ads should account for 30-50% of your entire ad budget *for all of the ads combined.* So, if you sponsor three products, each product will receive 1/3 of that total portion of your spending budget.

Sponsored Brand Ads

Sponsored brand ads appear the same way as sponsored product ads, and they work the same way, too. The only difference with a sponsored brand ad is that you are sponsoring your brand and not a specific product, so you are going to have only one single sponsored advertisement to reflect your entire brand.

Your sponsored brand ad will likely have a similar target audience as your product posts have, as your products and your brand itself will have the same audience. You can use the information you found from your sponsored product ads to determine the parameters of your sponsored brand ads.

When it comes to setting your budget for your sponsored brand ad, your brand ad should take 30-50% of your total advertising budget as well. This way, plenty of people are going to be exposed to your brand so that should they not find your product ads, they will find you.

Sponsored Display Ads

Sponsored display ads are the advertisements that appear on other people's websites, such as on blogs. Using sponsored display ads is a great way for you to reach other people's audiences so that you are more likely to drive traffic to your own page. You can create a sponsored display ad if you want to increase your reach with your Amazon store. However, the minimum budget for this option is generally $15,000, so it may be beyond most people's reach.

Creating a sponsored display ad is not done on your own, so if you want to use this feature, you will need to contact an Amazon ad consultant to be shown the process. A qualified consultant will help you determine if your budget is going to reasonably manage a display ad, and it will help you discover what the steps are for you to get your post sponsored in the first place.

Promoting Your Products

Promoting your products through paid advertisements is not the only way to get your name out there. Promoting your products on your own through word of mouth, known as organic advertising, is another powerful way for you to get your brand out there so that people can interact with your shop and purchase your products.

You should start organic advertising and product promotions at least two weeks before your products launch, as this gives you enough time to talk about your products and build your momentum. Generally, you can start your organic promotions as soon as your shipping procedures are finalized and paid for so that you can feel confident that everything will be in place for the launch date that you are giving your audience. You can promote your products organically on any social media platform through posting and talking about your products on a consistent basis.

The best way to really promote your products and brand this way is to take pictures of your sample products and talk about them and demonstrate them for your audience. As you do, focus on building engagement by asking questions and encouraging people to follow your page so that they can stay up to date on your launch. This way, they are able to get early access to your products the minute they land.

Reviewing Your Process

After you have launched your products, it is always a good idea to stop and review your launch process. Look over how each step of the process went and jot down any notes you have about how you could have made it go better or what you can do it make it smoother in the future. The more you can keep track and adapt this process to fulfill your own needs and understandings, the easier it is going to be for you to have a smooth launch process that works every single time. This way, launching becomes easier and easier, and your products sell out faster and faster. As a result, you will be earning a far higher income in the end.

Chapter 8: Growing Your Sales

After you launch your Amazon FBA storefront, you are going to want to place your entire focus on how you can achieve growth with your store. Growth is how you can ensure that you earn a great profit and that your profit continues to develop over time so that you can earn even more with your store.

Growth is a simple process overall, but it can feel challenging, especially for new business owners who are still trying to learn the ropes of their business. As I mentioned previously, one of the biggest elements of success and growth is momentum, as momentum will give you the opportunity to keep developing over time. Momentum is the positive forward motion that helps you grow and keep going, and it should never be overlooked when it comes to generating success with your business.

In business, momentum is the key to avoid getting forgotten about or having people fall off before you get the chance to really build your sales. With momentum, people get excited and curious, and that excitement and curiosity continue to grow over time until you launch your new products or sales, and they have the opportunity to buy something new from you. This energy is important as it is what will keep you going, so make sure that everything you do is with the intention to build your momentum and grow the energy of your business.

In addition to building your momentum, here are some other tips you can use to help you grow your sales and earn even more from your Amazon FBA business.

Focus On Your Rankings

First things first, you should always focus on your rankings when it comes to growing your Amazon FBA business. You want to focus on your product rankings and your seller ranking, as both of these are going to help you get in front of your audience in a bigger way.

With Amazon FBA, there is an e-mail sent out after products are purchased which encourages people to leave a review for your products. You are not going to need to do anything to encourage these. The same goes for your seller ranking, as people can rank both you and your store. Due to the nature of Amazon FBA, any reviews that complain about shipping or product management will not go toward your overall ranking as these are the responsibility of Amazon, not you.

What you can do to really contribute to your rankings improving is ensure that you are always offering the highest quality products possible and that your product descriptions are accurate so that people get exactly what they order. The more accurate and high quality you can make your shop and products, the more you are going to earn high-quality reviews that improve your rankings and help you sell more.

Do What You Know

When it comes to selling on Amazon FBA, you are already likely wandering in a world that you do not yet know much about. For that reason, it is a good idea to do what you know by sticking with your strengths and selling products that you understand. Doing so can ensure that you are not adding more stress into the learning process, which will help make the learning process go even smoother.

The best way to grow your business is to do what you know and teach yourself the most important basics, first. This way, everything you are learning and everything you are doing are familiar, and you have an easier time doing it well, which will only help your store grow larger and with greater integrity.

Always Track Your Numbers

We will discuss how you can monitor your growth and track your numbers in detail in Chapter 9. However, it is important to know that this is a crucial part of growing your business. Your numbers give you plenty of information about your business's productivity, what people like and what they want more of, and what you can do to improve your sales.

When people do not pay attention to their numbers, you can tell. Businesses fail when people are not watching the numbers because they do not have a clear idea of what is and what is not working. At the end of the day, all of the advice in the world will not give you a more accurate view of what you need to do to grow your business when compared to the actual numbers that you are receiving. Pay attention to them and use them accordingly, as this is your only way to track your momentum and guarantee your growth.

Grow Your Online Presence

If you really want to scale your business, you are going to have to run some form of an online presence. At the end of the day, Amazon is not going to turn as many eyes toward your store as you can until you have some of the best possible rankings all around. Even then, relying on Amazon is not necessarily the best way for you to really guarantee your growth.

A better way for you to grow your business and guarantee your growth is through establishing your own presence online and using your presence to help drive your traffic to your store. When you grow your own presence, you have greater control over getting your viewers to *your* store, rather than getting your viewers to Amazon central in general where you will then need to hope that they find your store.

You can grow your presence on Instagram, Facebook, Twitter, YouTube, and even Pinterest as a way to get your name out there. Growing your own blog is another great way to establish your brand and drive more traffic to your website so that you can improve your chances of getting found.

Use Paid Advertising

Paid advertising is an incredibly valuable way to grow your online presence. Although it does cost more this way, it will support you with getting seen by an audience that you may not necessarily see otherwise. As well, it automatically improves your ranking results by putting you right at the top of the listings rather than you having to rely on organic SEO alone to rank higher.

Even if you are not launching a new product, paying to sponsor your products and brand can go a long way in helping you get found by more people. If you really want to grow your Amazon FBA business, you should focus on having a monthly budget devoted exclusively to paid promotions. This way, you have plenty to help you continue promoting your products and getting a larger reach, thus improving your sales rankings.

Add More Products to Your Store

If you want to scale your business, one obvious way might be to add more products to your store. Having more products available for your customers to purchase means that you are more likely to have an increase in your sales because you are offering things that your audience actually wants to have more of.

When you are adding more products to your store, make sure that you are adding products that your customers actually want to buy. As well, make sure that every single product you sell makes sense to your brand and fits into your industry. This way, you are confident that your brand stays organized and relevant, and that it remains stocked with products that your customers are more likely to be interested in.

Chapter 9: Monitoring Your Amazon FBA Business

Monitoring your Amazon FBA business serves two important purposes: it prevents you from losing momentum, and it supports you with gaining growth. When you grow any business, paying attention to the numbers is a key opportunity for you to keep growing as it helps you get clear on where you are flourishing and where you are struggling to keep your business growing.

When it comes to monitoring your growth, it can be a challenge to know which numbers are important and which numbers are not exactly going to be necessary for helping your growth. In this chapter, I am going to tell you exactly what you need to pay attention to and how you can read it to make sure that you are getting the information that you need from your business so that you can effectively use that information for growth.

The Importance of Tracking Growth

Tracking your growth through your numbers is *crucial*. If you are not tracking your growth, you might begin to leak profits in big ways due to not having a clear understanding of what your business needs in order to actually grow effectively. For example, not tracking your numbers could lead to you not realizing that one of your products is not performing well which may lead to you adding more of that product to your stock, resulting in you holding onto a product that is not earning you a steady profit. Without tracking your numbers effectively, you could also engage in faulty marketing strategies, add the wrong products to your stock, or otherwise engage in behavior that is going to completely tank your growth.

When it comes to tracking your numbers for growth, it is important that you track your numbers effectively. This means that you should cultivate your own plan for how and when you are going to track your numbers so that you are staying consistent with them and tracking them effectively. A great system for tracking your numbers is to check in once each week, on the same day every week, and track all of your important numbers. Look them over and record them in a master leger so that you can look back over your numbers from time to time and see what your trends are. These trends are going to be crucial in helping you strategize your growth, so make sure that you remain consistent with them and track them effectively.

What Numbers To Pay Attention To

The numbers that you want to pay attention to when it comes to tracking your growth vary. Each of these numbers is going to serve your understanding in one way or another, so make sure that you effectively pay attention and get your numbers recorded properly.

The first numbers you want to pay attention to are the numbers around your sales. Pay attention to how many sales your store earned, and what products were sold in those sales. This way, you are able to clearly get a feel for what products are performing the best in your shop, and which ones are not performing as well.

You also want to pay attention to how many returns your products are getting. Comparing your returns to your sales will be a crucial measure for helping you determine the quality and popularity of your products, so keep track of these numbers, too.

Next, you want to pay attention to the metrics of who is actually purchasing your products. Amazon offers excellent information surrounding demographics, and this is going to be helpful in allowing you to determine whether or not you are effectively reaching the right demographic.

How to Use These Numbers for Product Growth

Tracking your numbers is virtually pointless if you have no idea how to use those numbers for growth. When it comes to using your numbers for growth, there is plenty of information that you gain from these numbers. These very numbers will tell you which products are performing best, which colors or customizations are performing best, which products are not performing well, and which products are not worth investing in anymore.

In a very basic sense, these numbers give you a clear idea as to which products you should purchase again and which products you can leave alone. Determining this is as simple as noting which products are selling in high quantities and which products are not selling very quickly at all. If you have products that are not selling quickly, naturally, you do not want to stock those products anymore. However, for the products that *are* selling quickly, you can go ahead and stock more of those products for your shop. These are products that are likely going to continue selling quickly.

The one time where you want to start being cautious about ordering more products that have been selling well is if you notice that the rate at which they are selling is steadily declining.

If you find that your sales are on a downtrend, you may not want to order as many units to avoid having the sales stop completely with you still having a large amount of stock in your possession. One strategy that people will do when they see a downtrend in sales is to stop stocking the product altogether for a while and leave it on "sold out." This way, they can build up a waitlist of people who want it before they bring more back into stock for their customers to sell.

Another way that you can use the numbers for product growth is to identify what types of products your customers like most so that you can use this information to determine which new products you are going to stock your store with. Generally, your numbers will show trends in what types of products your customers really like, and you can factor these numbers into the process of choosing your new products. This is a great opportunity for you to grow your business out in a direction that is going to carry on with the momentum that is already growing between you and your customers.

In addition to helping you pick new products altogether, using this information can help you determine what new variations or customizations you can offer with your products, too. If you find that purple and stripe prints tend to sell more than blue and circle prints, for example, you can stock more of your products in purple and find more unique stripe prints that people are more likely to purchase.

As you continue to follow the trends of your store, you will find that it becomes easier and easier for you to anticipate what your customers are going to want more of. This way, you can continue offering more of what they are actually going to purchase and stocking less in terms of products that are not really selling well or not really appealing to your existing audience.

How to Use These Numbers for Volume Growth

In addition to helping you determine what products to stock your store with, your numbers can help you grow your volume of sales, too. The easiest way to use your numbers to fuel growth in your sales volumes is through identifying which of your products are most popular and then placing all of your marketing efforts and initiatives into those products. Since these products are already thriving, adding more efforts into your promotions will result in even more units selling, which will result in your higher volumes.

A great way to keep your volume ratio up when it comes to promoting these individual products that are selling best is to really place all of your promotional efforts here. Focus on sharing about these products on your social media platforms, get influencers using your products and promoting them for you, and focus most of your paid promotion budget on promoting these products. This is how you are really going to ramp up your attention being directed on these products to help you succeed in improving your volume sales.

When you plan to increase volume sales in certain products, it is crucial that you make sure that you keep that product in stock at Amazon's warehouse. If you run out of product even for a short period of time, you may lose your momentum as people seek out another shop to keep their products stocked through. Because of how stocked you have to keep the warehouse. However, it is crucial that you pay close attention to your ongoing number trends. If you find that your numbers begin to dip, you need to reduce the volume of product you are keeping stock at Amazon's warehouse to avoid being left with too many products that will ultimately move much slower than the initial wave.

Chapter 10: Secrets and Tips for Your Success

Every single new venture you take in life is going to come with lessons that you can only gain through hands-on experience. However, I want to help you gain this experience and grow faster by having an awareness of what lessons you are likely going to learn about and face in your Amazon FBA business.

In this chapter, I have provided you with five of the most important secrets and tips that you need to succeed that typically will only be discovered by those who are experiencing their businesses hands-on. Use these to help you get a jump-start and launch your business ahead of where most people launch, as this will give you the best opportunity to really help your business blow up right away.

Always Focus On Your Competitive Edge

When it comes to launching a business, focusing on your competitive edge is crucial. Your competitive edge is your opportunity to really create the opportunity to set yourself apart from other Amazon FBA merchants so that customers are more likely to choose you over anyone else. Understand that no matter where or how you are promoting yourself, whether it is exclusively through Amazon or through Amazon as well as social media, other people are trying to access your clients, too. This means that you need to really know where your competitive edge lies and promote that competitive edge while also nurturing it so that you continue to remain competitive.

Learning how to nurture and promote your competitive edge requires some practice, especially if you have never run a business in the first place. To help you get started, let's explore what your competitive edge is, how you can promote it, and how you can nurture this edge so that no one comes in and sharpens your edge better than you do.

The first step in using your competitive edge to your advantage is knowing what your competitive edge is. Your competitive edge is the element of your business that sets you apart from your competition in a way that makes you better than they are. If you really focus on developing and refining your business, chances are you are going to have multiple competitive edges over many of your competitors. So, when it comes to the competitive edge that is going to set you apart and help you grow, you want to focus on the competitive edge that your customers actually care about.

For example, maybe you are better are supplying more colors and customizations than your competition is. Or, maybe you are better at providing items that are trending right as they start to get popular, which is an excellent competitive edge. These types of competitive edges are things that your customers will actually care about and want to learn more about. Avoid talking about competitive edges like "we have the best tracking system for organizing our products" or "we are the best at sourcing products for cheap" because these are not something that many of your customers are going to care about. Unless, of course, you are selling to people who are buying bulk products and who want the best deals and the best quality products, in which case this is a perfect competitive edge!

Once you identify what your competitive edge is, you need to nurture this edge by ensuring that everything you do in your business keeps this edge sharp. This means that if your competitive edge is always having the lowest product pricing, you always need to be looking for the best deals that help you keep your sales prices lower than the market average. Keeping your competitive edge nurtured in this way will ensure that it always remains your competitive edge, which will help you become known for this. People will start to rave about you being the best because of this, which will improve your brand recognition and help you grow your business even larger.

Because your competitive edge is going to be so key in helping you sell your products, you want to find a way to work it into your brand. You can do this by creating a motto or a slogan that promotes your competitive edge and then regularly saying and using that slogan in your marketing so that people come to know you for it. For example, McDonald's strives to be the restaurant that people go to for a family experience that is enjoyable and that always tastes good, and so their slogan is "I'm lovin' it." Alternatively, Lays brands themselves as being the chip brand that you are going to want to eat constantly and that you will struggle to stop with because they taste so good. For that reason, their slogan is "Bet you can't have just one." These slogans directly market their competitive edge, making it easier for you to know exactly why you would want to purchase these brands over any of their competitors.

Create a Strong Customer Experience

When it comes to running any form of business, having a strong customer experience is important. When it comes to retail, your customer experience is not going to be as involved as the experience of someone purchasing a service. However, there are still plenty of opportunities for you to create a custom and enjoyable customer experience.

A common misbelief that people have when they launch their Amazon FBA businesses is that they are not going to have to deal with their customer experience at all. With Amazon managing your storefront and your shipping and fulfillment processes, it can be easy to assume that there is no way for you to have any way to customize your customer experience. However, that is simply not true.

Creating a strong customer experience can be done by really considering what the process is going to be like for your customer from the moment they learn about the brand to the moment that your product reaches their hands and they begin using it. Being mindful about this entire experience will give you the opportunity to create an experience that is going to be enjoyable and memorable. As well, because you took the opportunity to create an experience that stands out in the first place, you will set yourself apart from other Amazon merchants, helping you stand out against the crowd and improving your competitive edge even more.

With Amazon, the best way to create a great customer experience is to consider what your branding and promotions look like. Believe it or not, these are a largely relevant part of your customer experience, and doing them right is the best opportunity that you have to set yourself apart from others. You can customize your experience by creating graphics and descriptions of your products that are branded and that are enjoyable to read and engage with. This way, when people see your products and begin to read about them, they begin to generate excitement, and it becomes an experience for them.

Another great way to improve your customer experience is to offer high-quality products that are better than anything else on the market. Through this, every time they receive one of your products they are going to have fun opening it and using it because they can feel confident that it is going to be high quality and worth the investment. If you can work together with the supplier to create a more enjoyable experience by including branded inserts in your boxes that describe or explain the product, this is another great way to improve your customer experience.

You can also improve your customer experience outside of Amazon. Leverage your social media platforms as an opportunity to shine a spotlight on people who purchase your products by sharing their posts, commenting on their posts, and otherwise engaging with them. Doing this can help you really get in front of your audience and show them that they are valued and that you appreciate their loyalty. As a result, you create a fun and enjoyable experience that helps your customers feel like they are a part of something bigger.

Leverage Your Descriptions

Your descriptions are a wonderful opportunity for you to really boost your sales. On Amazon, many people open stores and upload generic, pre-written descriptions that are fairly boring. These descriptions are often direct and clear. However, they lack any personality and fail to really represent your brand or create something memorable for your customer.

To leverage your descriptions, all you have to do is customize your descriptions so that they are both accurate *and* enjoyable to read. Show your brand's personality in the descriptions by using words that are relevant to your brand and speaking in a way that is relevant to your audience. Using the same slang and words that they would use is a great opportunity for you to connect with your audience in a way that they understand and relate to, which helps you stand out even further.

Although you do not have a large space to work within your descriptions, you can still make them fun and enjoyable. Get creative and always use this as an opportunity to make a stand-out experience for your customers with your brand.

Learn To Take Better Pictures

When it comes to your Amazon listings, having the right pictures is crucial. Many people on Amazon upload generic pictures of their photographs that are taken from the suppliers and use these as their listings. Although these photographs work, they are not going to help you stand apart from everyone else that is selling products just like yours. In order to really stand out, you are going to want to use the sample products you received to take your pictures for Amazon.

There are a few key approaches that you can use to help you get a high-quality photograph for your listing. The first one is to remember that all of the best pictures follow a minimalist approach, as this supports your viewers with knowing exactly what you are selling. If you have too much going on in your picture, it can look overwhelming and draw eyes away, or it can cause people to wonder what exactly they are going to be purchasing from you.

You also want to make sure that your pictures have good lighting and are clear. Attempting to show pictures that have poor lighting or that are blurry is only going to result in people overlooking your posts and choosing something else instead. You can easily invest in an inexpensive ring light from Amazon as well as a decent quality camera that is going to help you capture the products in high def. These days, most smartphones shoot photographs in 4K quality, meaning that you can likely use your phone to shoot the photographs for your image. Just make sure that you hold your hand steady and that you activate the 4K shooting quality so that your image appears in high def.

If you are unsure about how you can photograph your products effectively, consider looking on the search results for listings where other individuals have clearly taken their own photographs. Pay attention to how they have done it, what they have focused on, and the focus of their pictures so that you can get a better feel for what you are looking for in your own pictures, helping you get inspired to take the right photographs.

Engage With Reviewers When Necessary

Although Amazon is going to handle most of your customer care inquiries, it does not hurt to engage with some of them on your own as well. You can engage with reviewers easily by simply going onto your page, identifying what people are saying about your products, and writing back. Do not be afraid to leave comments like "thank you for your review!" under the comments that are positive and that are encouraging other people to purchase your products. If you find that people are leaving low-quality reviews, avoid getting defensive. Instead, ask them what they would like to see more of and how the experience could have been better. If it was something you can fix on your own, such as by finding a new supplier or making adjustments to your products or listings, do that. If it was something that needed to be managed by Amazon, ensure that your product reviewer has the right information to get in touch with Amazon so that they can receive support and have a more positive experience.

Although you do not have to do this, taking the time to engage on your own is going to help you have a more personal and positive impact in your business. You are also going to have the unique opportunity to see where you can improve on your service so that everyone has a positive experience with your shop. Through your own reviews, you can learn more about what new customizations and variations should be considered, what other products you can share, and how you can continue offering great quality. Never overlook the value of spending time reading your own reviews for support in growing your business on Amazon FBA.

Chapter 11: Amazon FBA and Tax Season

Amazon FBA is a business that will require you to file taxes. You might be wondering how you can file taxes with Amazon FBA, including what tax forms you will need and what you need to track in order to submit your taxes clearly and precisely. In this chapter, we are going to summarize what needs to be done come tax season for you to properly file your Amazon FBA business so that you are compliant with what is required of you as a business owner.

When it comes to filing taxes for your Amazon FBA business, it is truly not that challenging. If you have ever filed as a self-employed individual before, you will be pleased to find that it is not much different than filing for your own business. If you are new to filing for yourself, you might want to book with a tax agent who can help you file your taxes properly so that you do not make any mistakes in your filing process.

Using the Amazon 1099-K Tax Form

1099-K tax forms are forms that help the IRS know how much money you have made monthly, as well as annually, through your business. Individuals who are filing on their own will often file 1099-K forms to track their income through their own businesses. Fortunately for you, Amazon also uses the 1099-K to track information relating to sales, taxes, and shipping fees. This means that if you are a professional seller who is selling large quantities of products through Amazon, your form will already be filled out through Amazon's employees as they manage your products. All you have to do, then, is print off the 1099-K and use it to file your taxes.

If you are an individual seller, or if you do not make a significant amount through your business in any given year, chances are you will not receive a 1099-K because you did not make enough money through your business to file it. For the 1099-K, there is a threshold of $20,000 that needs to be met in order for Amazon to fill it out. If you do not meet that threshold, Amazon will not fill it out for you, and you will not receive one.

It is important to realize that if you have more than $20,000 in sales, Amazon will be filing a 1099-K form for your business, which means the IRS already knows that you have a business with Amazon. If you fail to report this income or if you report it incorrectly, you could be audited due to your discrepancy. Pay attention and make sure that your numbers match the ones on the 1099-K generated by Amazon so that you do not find yourself being audited.

As well, even if you do not receive a 1099-K, you still must file taxes on all of the income that you received from Amazon. It will still count toward your overall annual income, and it just won't qualify you for a 1099-K to be filled out and provided to you from Amazon.

What Qualifies As Income

The IRS is going to track your gross annual income through Amazon, which is going to include everything that you earned, including your revenue, not just your profits. Any numbers relating to your income, including shipping charges and anything else you receive, are all going to be listed on your 1099-K, even if you did not receive all of these funds directly into your bank account.

If you are not sure about the numbers, or if you have never filed this way before, filing with a consultant can help you keep track of your numbers more effectively so that you do not make any mistakes and pay for it later on. Always trust the numbers that come in on your 1099-K because, at the end of the day, Amazon was responsible for helping you with all of the income, which means that their state-of-the-art systems are likely more accurate than your own.

Reporting Income Outside the US

If you are selling on Amazon outside of the US, you are not liable for US taxes, which means that you are not going to receive a 1099-K form from Amazon. What you will need to do is provide a W-8BEN form to Amazon which is going to exempt Amazon from having to report your income for tax purposes.

For anyone selling outside of the US, you are going to have to track your own income and file according to your country's unique tax laws. Again, it is still important that you report and pay taxes on your Amazon income as not doing so could result in serious penalties for lying on your taxes.

Tracking Amazon Tax Deductions

Anyone who runs their own business qualifies for certain tax deductions throughout the year. Typically, any expense that contributes to you running your own business is going to be considered a tax deduction, so it is important that you keep all of your receipts relating to your business. Keep receipts from everyone, such as your suppliers, your shipping companies, Amazon, and any promotional or marketing expenses that you pay. Anything that directly contributes to you making an income on Amazon can be considered a tax deduction, so feel free to note this down in your taxes.

It is important that you keep the receipts for any tax deduction that you make on your business. Receipts provide evidence that these funds were spent and that you did put the money toward running your business. If you do not have them, even if the money was spent on your business, you might run into problems later on should the IRS decide to audit you. Avoid these problems by keeping your business receipts for seven years so that any audits made are able to be proven and reported through your saved receipts.

Conclusion

Amazon FBA is an incredible business model that has the capacity to allow everyday people to get into a profitable home-based business for relatively cheap. Due to the improved services being made available by both Amazon and suppliers like Alibaba, getting involved in a business like this is easier than ever before.

If you want to open your own business and start earning money in a way that is fairly easy to learn, Amazon FBA is definitely worth considering. Depending on how you want to run your business, you can be as hands-off or hands-on as you want with Amazon FBA. You can choose to have Amazon completely run everything by having them manage fulfillment and paying them to manage your advertisements if you wanted. In this case, all you would have to do is purchase products and upload your product descriptions, as well as manage your advertisements. Or, if you wanted to be more hands-on, you could take advantage of all of these features and run your own organic promotional efforts through social media. There truly is no limit on how you can run your business and how involved or passive it can be.

One of the greatest things about Amazon FBA is that it is a business that you can start on the side of whatever else you are doing in your life. Because so much of the heavy lifting is being done by Amazon, you can begin your business while you are still working full-time elsewhere or even while you are running your own business completely separate of your Amazon FBA business. The versatility here is incredible and offers the opportunity for many people to shift their income from being primarily linear or earned from a job to being primarily online or earned through Amazon FBA. Many people even quit their jobs and other businesses entirely as they earn $10,000+ per month through Amazon FBA, which results in them not truly having to do anything else anyway.

If you still feel confident that Amazon FBA is for you, you now have all of the direction that you need to get started with your Amazon FBA business. Simply go back to the beginning of this book and read through, following the process step-by-step this time to help you get started. As long as you follow these exact steps, you will have a thriving Amazon FBA business in no time.

If this is your second time reading through this book and you have already followed the steps, I want to congratulate you! You are taking huge steps in achieving financial independence through your own business, and that is something well worth celebrating. Continue to follow these same steps while also educating yourself on how you can do even better, and you can feel confident that your business is going to grow rapidly.

Before you go, I want to ask you if you could please consider reviewing this book. The more feedback I gain from readers just like you, the more I can offer similar products and services that are going to help you in your goal of becoming financially independent. Your feedback is greatly appreciated!

Lastly, I want to say thank you for reading *Amazon FBA 2019*. I hope it has helped you in feeling confident in mastering your Amazon FBA business.

Best of luck in your successful venture!

Made in the USA
Monee, IL
20 January 2020

20591697R00072